The INSIDE GUIDE

CELEBRATING NATIVE AMERICAN CULTURES

Native American Governments

By Trisha James

Cavendish Square

New York

Published in 2023 by Cavendish Square Publishing, LLC
29 East 21st Street New York, NY 10010

Website: cavendishsq.com

This publication represents the opinions and views of the author based on his or her personal experience, knowledge, and research. The information in this book serves as a general guide only. The author and publisher have used their best efforts in preparing this book and disclaim liability rising directly or indirectly from the use and application of this book.

Disclaimer: Portions of this work were originally authored by Sarah Machajewski and published as *Native American Governments: From Tribal Councils to Constitutions* (Native American Cultures). All new material this edition authored by Trisha James.

All websites were available and accurate when this book was sent to press.

Cataloging-in-Publication Data

Names: James, Trisha.
Title: Native American governments / Trisha James.
Description: New York : Cavendish Square Publishing, 2023. | Series: The inside guide: celebrating Native American cultures | Includes glossary and index. Identifiers: ISBN 9781502664204 (pbk.) | ISBN 9781502664228 (library bound) | ISBN 9781502664211 (6-pack) | ISBN 9781502664235 (ebook) Subjects: LCSH: Indians of North America–Politics and government–Juvenile literature. | Indians of North America–Kings and rulers–Juvenile literature.Classification: LCC E98.T77 J36 2023 | DDC 970.004'97–dc23

Editor: Therese Shea
Copyeditor: Jill Keppeler
Designer: Deanna Paternostro

Some of the images in this book illustrate individuals who are models. The depictions do not imply actual situations or events.

CPSIA compliance information: Batch #CSCSQ23: For further information contact Cavendish Square Publishing LLC, New York, New York, at 1-877-980-4450.

Printed in the United States of America

Find us on

CONTENTS

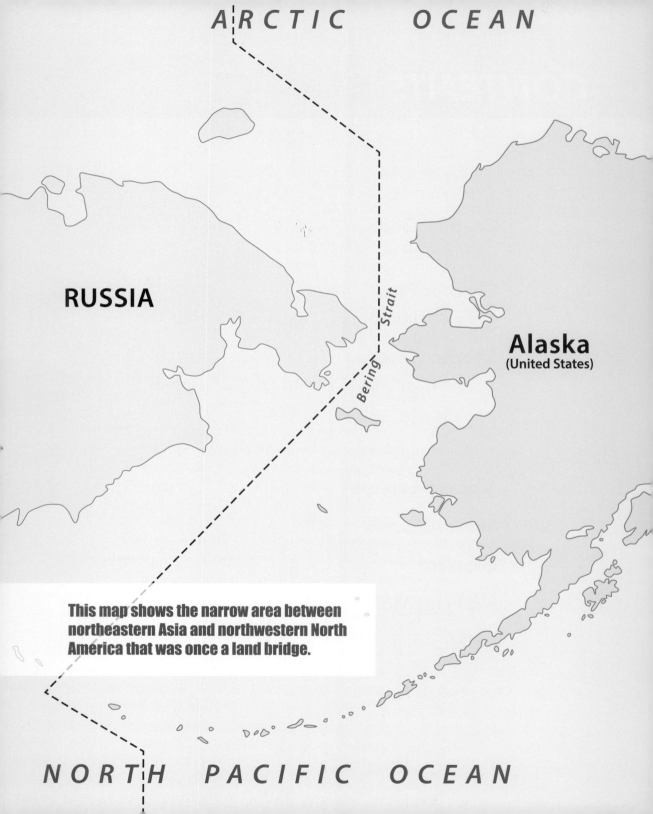

ARCTIC OCEAN

RUSSIA

Bering Strait

Alaska
(United States)

This map shows the narrow area between
northeastern Asia and northwestern North
America that was once a land bridge.

NORTH PACIFIC OCEAN

Chapter One

THE FIRST AMERICANS

Modern humans first came from Africa. They spread from there across Europe and Asia. They reached central Asia and the area that's now Siberia in Russia about 40,000 years ago. From there, they likely crossed into North America.

In the United States, Indigenous peoples—the first peoples to live there—are often called Native Americans. It's widely believed that the **ancestors** of today's Native Americans came to North America more than 13,000 years ago. Many think they traveled into the Americas from Siberia on foot, using a small strip of land between the continents sometimes called a land bridge. Today, this area is covered by a narrow body of water called the Bering Strait. Over thousands of years, different groups of people moved and settled around the Americas.

Fast Fact

The Indigenous peoples of North America are often called Native Americans, American Indians, and First Peoples (especially in Canada). While this book mostly uses "Native American," different communities prefer different terms.

Cultures Separate

Many Native groups lost contact with each other as they moved across North America. Slowly, separate **cultures** developed,

5

The Hunkpapa Lakota chief Sitting Bull tried to stop U.S. invaders from taking over his people's traditional lands in the late 1800s.

each with their own ways of life. Communities needed leadership, which, for many, meant the rise of governments. At first, every adult in a group likely had a voice in making decisions. Later, as separate but related groups wanted to work together, more complicated kinds of governments arose.

Traditional Native American governments differed among cultures. Sometimes elders—the respected older people of the community—appointed leaders. Some leaders were born into the position. Native American leaders made decisions and established rules their people followed. Native Americans have had courageous leaders to guide them through hard times, especially after Europeans came to the Americas desiring land, resources, and power over the Native peoples.

EARLY GOVERNMENTS

In early Native American societies, the basic group was the family. Families sometimes joined together to share the burden of more difficult tasks such as hunting, farming, and defending themselves. Larger groups survived more easily. Several extended families sometimes formed groups called bands. Historians think that in small social units like these, nearly all adults took part in decisions affecting the band. They also think a male, perhaps the best hunter, may have acted as the band's leader, but only according to the group's demands. This person may have represented the band in dealing with other groups of Native Americans, for example.

Different and Alike

When Europeans arrived in North America in the 1500s, people of many different cultures were already living there. Europeans didn't think these Native Americans were much like them at first. They spoke different languages, wore different clothes, and had different ways of life from them—often hunting and gathering their food, for example. However, Europeans and Native peoples were alike in some ways too. Rule by government was one thing they had in common.

Europeans soon learned that Native Americans lived in societies with traditions, laws, and governing bodies, as they did. After the U.S. government was established, it recognized many Native groups as

Leaders of the Confederated Salish and Kootenai Tribes of the Flathead Nation of Washington State surround U.S. Secretary of the Interior Harold Ickes as he approves their constitution in 1935.

Fast Fact

For many years, the United States tried to make Native Americans more like white Americans, a process called assimilation.

independent nations at first. Later, though, countless Native Americans were pushed from their lands to make way for white settlers. Many had to rebuild their communities and cultures in other places and fight to have their governments recognized once more.

In 1934, the Indian Reorganization Act, passed by the U.S. Congress, decreased the federal government's control of Native American matters and increased Native American self-government.

Wampum belts, made of tiny shells, recorded Haudenosaunee laws, traditions, and history. The design of the Hiawatha Belt represents the formation of the Haudenosaunee Confederacy. Today, the group uses the design on its flag, shown here.

The Haudenosaunee, sometimes called the Iroquois, are often thought of and honored for having America's earliest democracy. A democracy is a kind of government in which the people hold the power. People may participate in the decisions of the government directly or indirectly, often through representatives whom they've elected. An indirect democracy has allowed the Haudenosaunee to maintain a strong **alliance** for hundreds of years and has had a direct effect on the history of the United States.

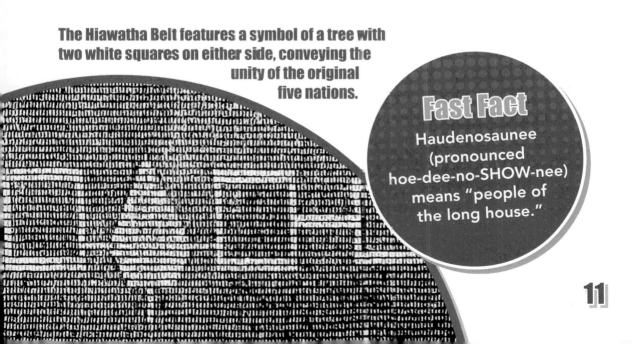

The Hiawatha Belt features a symbol of a tree with two white squares on either side, conveying the unity of the original five nations.

Fast Fact

Haudenosaunee (pronounced hoe-dee-no-SHOW-nee) means "people of the long house."

The Six Nations

Between 1570 and 1600, the Haudenosaunee formed a confederacy first made up of representatives from five nations: the Seneca, Mohawk, Oneida, Onondaga, and Cayuga. A sixth nation, the Tuscarora, joined them in 1722.

Also called the Six Nations, the Haudenosaunee Confederacy was led by a Grand Council made up of 50 leaders called *hoyaneh*. Everyone had a vote, but all 50 had to come to a consensus, or agreement, to make decisions.

Today, the Grand Council of the Haudenosaunee Confederacy is still a working government. It's the oldest government in its original form in North America. The modern council continues to settle arguments and makes decisions to benefit the whole alliance. These decisions must agree with the Gayanesshagowa, or Great Law of Peace, which is the Haundenosaunee Confederacy's constitution.

The three main ideas of the Great Law are **righteousness**, justice, and health. The Great Law instructs the Haudenosaunee on preserving their democracy and expresses how reason is important to maintain peace. Among other points, the Great Law of Peace states that all Haudenosaunee people have rights and their leaders are meant to serve the people.

Fast Fact

According to the Haudenosaunee, a Huron named Dekanawidah (or the Peacemaker) and Onondaga chief Hiawatha presented the Great Law of Peace to the original five nations of the confederacy.

CLAN MOTHERS

Women called clan mothers hold an important role in the Haudenosaunee Confederacy and its government. Each of the confederacy's nations is made up of groups of families called clans. The clan chooses a clan mother based on a woman's wisdom and commitment to her culture. She serves as clan mother for life. Her roles include making decisions for her clan, naming the people in her clan, and selecting men to serve on the Grand Council. These men can serve on the council for life, but if they're not acting in the best interests of the nations, the clan mothers can remove them.

Representatives from the Onondaga, one of the six nations of the Haudenosaunee Confederacy, attend a conference in Washington, D.C., to speak about issues important to their people.

"No state, nor person, can purchase your lands, unless at some public treaty, held under the authority of the United States. The General Government will never consent to your being defrauded, but will protect you in all your just rights."

– President George Washington

Wilma Mankiller was the first woman to serve as the principal chief of the Cherokee Nation. Here, she accepts the Presidential Medal of Freedom from President Bill Clinton.

14

The Cherokee

When Europeans arrived in North America, the Cherokee lived in the Southeast. They were one of the largest politically connected groups of Native Americans, perhaps numbering as many as 22,500 people in the mid-1600s. Each Cherokee town had a council house in which all adults, including women, made important decisions.

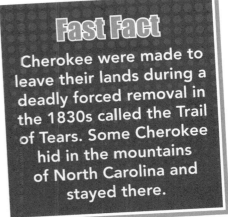

Fast Fact

Cherokee were made to leave their lands during a deadly forced removal in the 1830s called the Trail of Tears. Some Cherokee hid in the mountains of North Carolina and stayed there.

As white settlers moved onto Cherokee lands, the Native Americans adopted some practices of white culture, such as a written constitution, hoping they'd be allowed to remain on their lands. Most were still forced to relocate.

Today, there are three **federally recognized** Cherokee tribes: the Cherokee Nation of Oklahoma, the United Keetoowah Band in Oklahoma, and the Eastern Band of Cherokee Indians in North Carolina. The Cherokee Nation is the largest of these, with more than 390,000 members. Many live in Oklahoma, where a **reservation** was established for them in the 1800s. The Cherokee Nation's government is made up of three branches, including a chief, council, and courts, and is based on a constitution ratified, or approved, by the people.

Strong chiefs such as Washakie of the Eastern Band of Wyoming Shoshone were needed to stand up to the U.S. government's policies. They were the voice of their people.

MORE CULTURES, COUNCILS, AND COMMITTEES

Chapter Three

The Haudenosaunee and Cherokee aren't the only peoples governed by a council of leaders. In fact, a tribal council guided by a constitution oversees most Native American groups. Some elected Native leaders have the title of chairperson, chief, president, or governor. Native governments often include court systems with appointed or elected judges too. However, the historical experiences of each Native group differ, as did the development of their governments.

The Shoshone People

The Shoshones were located in California, Montana, Nevada, Utah, Wyoming, and Idaho. They were never united under a single government. Some bands were led by a *daigwahni* (chief), who controlled the community's movements and hunting practices. Sometimes councils selected this leader. A different chief might be selected in a time of war. Other bands were governed by councils of family leaders and warriors.

Fast Fact

Washakie was a respected chief in the mid-1800s. He was the only Native American leader honored with a U.S. military funeral.

Today, a council elected by the people and guided by a constitution leads most Shoshone groups. For example, the Fort Hall Business Council governs the Shoshone-Bannock of Idaho, and the Shoshone-Paiute Tribal Business Council governs the Shoshone-Paiute of Idaho and Nevada. A chairman heads both of these councils.

The Pueblo Peoples

The Pueblo cultures of Arizona and New Mexico include the Hopi and Zuni peoples. Long ago, Pueblo villages were independent and governed by religious councils. Each clan sent a representative to the council, which met in kivas, or special rooms built under the ground.

Fast Fact

In 1620, the Spanish directed that Native governors should rule Pueblo communities (though the Spanish had ultimate authority). These leaders were given silver-headed canes.

People have lived in Taos Pueblo, New Mexico, for more than 1,000 years.

Pueblo leaders in Washington, D.C., in 1923 protest a bill that would have given their lands to white settlers. The bill was defeated.

Today, local governments still lead many Pueblo communities. Twenty Pueblo governors meet as part of the All Pueblo Council of Governors, which traces its roots to 1598. The organization focuses on land and water rights, education, health-care issues, and economic opportunities.

The Plains Peoples

The Native Americans of the Plains include many peoples, such as the Pawnee, Sioux, Blackfoot, and Cheyenne. Government within most **nomadic** Plains communities existed at the band level. A band consisted of dozens to hundreds of people and could grow bigger and smaller at times. Leaders, or headmen, had to prove themselves worthy of their role through their bravery and wisdom. Groups called military societies within a band kept order and enforced decisions. At one time, the Cheyenne had 10 bands and sent representatives from each to a council of 44 peace chiefs. The decrees, or rulings, of this council applied to the whole people.

Today, the Cheyenne and Arapaho peoples are federally recognized as one tribe, which now lives in Oklahoma after being pushed from their

THE INUIT

The Inuit people have survived in the Arctic for at least 3,800 years. Inuit live in Alaska, Canada, Greenland, and eastern Russia. Traditionally, they lived in family communities without official governments. The Inuit began working toward building a government in the late 1960s. They wanted control over lands and issues such as education and health care.

Nunatsiavut is the first Inuit region in Canada to achieve self-government, though it's still a part of Newfoundland and Labrador. However, the Nunatsiavut government, operating under the Labrador Inuit Constitution, maintains authority over culture, health, education, justice, and other matters for its people.

The Nunatsiavut Assembly Building is the home of the Nunatsiavut Assembly, the legislative body.

traditional lands. Their tribal council includes all members of the tribe 18 years old or older. They also have an executive branch led by a governor, a legislative branch, and a court system including a supreme court.

Beginning in 2016, the Standing Rock Sioux government protested the construction of the Dakota Access oil pipeline (DAPL) across their lands.

The Treaty of Fort Laramie of 1868 made the Black Hills, shown here, part of the Great Sioux Reservation. In 1877, the U.S. government seized the Black Hills of South Dakota after gold was found there.

SOVEREIGN NATIONS

Native American governments were especially needed during times in U.S. history when the American government didn't recognize Native peoples' right to govern themselves. U.S. policies separated communities and even families and tried to force Native Americans to desert traditions.

Native leadership helped groups survive hardships until the United States finally agreed these groups could have self-government as independent states, known as sovereignty. However, even when the United States established treaties, or formal agreements, with sovereign Native nations, sometimes it didn't honor the treaties.

Fast Fact

In 1980, the U.S. Supreme Court awarded the Sioux $102 million for the Black Hills territory they lost in the 1800s. The Sioux refused the money and are still hoping for their land back.

Broken Treaties

From 1778 to 1871, the United States signed more than 360 treaties with Indigenous groups, many promising protection of Native territory and resources. However, as the country expanded westward, white Americans moved west—often onto Native American lands. This, among other events such as the discovery of gold and other valuable resources on these lands, led to broken treaties.

Some Native American governments today are seeking **reparations** for past broken treaties. Some have had success through the U.S. Supreme Court. In 1986, the Ute Indian Tribe of Utah received 3 million acres (1.2 million hectares) of land that had been taken in the early 1900s by the U.S. government.

Recognition

In 1988, U.S. Congress honored the Haudenosaunee (calling them the Iroquois) with a **resolution** and noted that Founding Fathers George Washington and Benjamin Franklin greatly admired them. American lawmakers recognized the Haudenosaunee as well as other Native American nations contributed to the formation of the United States, noting the "confederation of the original 13 colonies" was "influenced by the political system developed by the Iroquois Confederacy."

NATIVE AMERICANS IN U.S. GOVERNMENT

In the 2020 U.S. elections, a record number of Native American candidates won seats in the House of Representatives and Senate. Fourteen candidates ran for national office, and six were elected. A number of states reported a record number of Native American voters.

Deb Haaland, a member of the Pueblo of Laguna, is one of the first Native American women to serve in Congress as a representative. She became the first Native American to be a cabinet secretary when she was sworn in as secretary of the interior in 2021. This position oversees the management and **conservation** of federal lands and natural resources.

THE WHITE HOUSE
WASHINGTON

Haaland told the website *Indian Country Today*, "We need to be where folks are making decisions. We need to be a voice at the table, regardless of what table it is but making decisions for our people, for our **constituents**, for our country."

25

The resolution further stated that the United States has a "government-to-government relationship with Indian tribes" and must "exercise good faith in upholding its treaties" with them.

Self-Government

As of 2021, there are 574 federally recognized tribes in the United States. Becoming a federally recognized tribe is a years-long process. Sometimes being federally recognized means having a government different than what a people might prefer. For example, the Navajo of the Southwest historically preferred local clan governments, but federal recognition requires them to have a strong central government. Still, it's important to the nation to have the final decision about issues affecting its people's well-being.

No one knows the issues of Native peoples better than Native Americans themselves, and their governments work hard to address serious problems that Native Americans face on reservations, such as poverty, unemployment, and poor health care. Improving the lives of their people continues to be a top concern for all Native American governments.

Another issue facing Native American groups is the education of their young people in their traditions and languages. Some Native languages are no longer spoken.

MORE TO EXPLORE

The Three Largest Native American Tribes

People	Population	Features of Government	Official Website
Navajo Nation	399,500*	president, council, court system	www.navajo-nsn.gov/
Cherokee Nation	392,000*	principal chief, tribal council, court system	www.cherokee.org/
Choctaw Nation of Oklahoma	204,000**	tribal chief, council, court system	www.choctawnation.com/

*enrolled members as of 2020
**enrolled members as of 2021

1. Why do you think it was harder for Indigenous peoples organized as bands to unite under a single government?

2. Can you think of any advantages of consensus decision-making by the Haudenosaunee Grand Council as opposed to majority decision-making?

3. Do you think the United States should acknowledge more past broken treaties with Native American groups? Why or why not?

4. Why do you think it's necessary for Native Americans to have self-government and also representation in U.S. government?

GLOSSARY

alliance: A union between groups or people.

ancestor: A person in someone's family who lived in past times.

confederacy: Two or more groups in an agreement of support.

conservation: The care of the natural world.

constituent: One who lives and votes in an area.

constitution: The basic laws by which a country or state is governed.

culture: The beliefs and ways of life of a group of people.

federally recognized: Having a special relationship with the U.S. government, which has responsibilities, powers, and limitations attached to it.

nomadic: Having to do with people who move from place to place.

reparation: Something done or given to correct a mistake.

reservation: Land set aside by the U.S. government for Native Americans.

resolution: A formal declaration stating feelings or decisions of a group.

righteousness: The state of following religious or moral laws.

FIND OUT MORE

Books

Machajewski, Sarah. *The Real Story Behind U.S. Treaties with Native Americans*. New York, NY: PowerKids Press, 2020.

Morlock, Theresa. *Inside the Native American Rights Movement*. New York, NY: Gareth Stevens Publishing, 2018.

Websites

Cherokee Nation
www.cherokee.org/
Learn more about one of the largest Native populations in the United States today.

Native American Facts for Kids
www.native-languages.org/kids.htm
This site offers links about Native American history to students of all ages.

United South and Eastern Tribes
www.usetinc.org/
Learn about this partnership among 33 U.S. tribes, who find "strength in unity."

INDEX